AF489325

YELLOW ANIMALS ON THE PLANET

Speedy Publishing LLC
40 E. Main St. #1156
Newark, DE 19711
www.speedypublishing.com

Copyright 2015

All Rights reserved. No part of this book may be reproduced or used in any way or form or by any means whether electronic or mechanical, this means that you cannot record or photocopy any material ideas or tips that are provided in this book

The plant and animal kingdoms
abound with bright colors. Color plays
a multitude of roles in the natural
world, used to entice, to camouflage,
or to warn other creatures.

YELLOW WARBLER

are uniformly yellow birds. Yellow Warblers are small, evenly proportioned songbirds with medium-length tails and rounded heads. Yellow Warblers breed in shrubby thickets and woods, particularly along watercourses and in wetlands.

YELLOW TANG

is one of the most popular aquarium fish. Yellow tang are bright yellow in color. The Yellow Tang has a disk like shaped body similar to all surgeonfish, but with large dorsal and anal fins.

YELLOW JACKET

is the common name
in North America
for predatory wasps.
Yellow Jackets are
yellow and black with
stripes or bands on
their abdomen. Yellow
Jackets primarily eat
fruit and plant nectar.

LARGE GRASS YELLOW BUTTERFLY

is a small pierid butterfly species found in Asia or Africa. Common Grass Yellow butterflies are bright lemon yellow in colour, and have black markings at the tips. Common Grass Yellow butterflies like to fly quickly, close to the ground and are found in open grassy or bushy terrain.

GOLDEN POISON FROG

is the most lethal of the poison dart frogs and is considered the most poisonous animal on earth. The golden poison frog is diurnal, meaning it is active during the day.

AMERICAN GOLDFINCH

is a small finch with
a short, conical
bill. It has a small,
head, long wings,
and short, notched
tail. The goldfinch s
main natural habitats
are weedy fields
and floodplains,
where plants such as
thistles and asters are
common.

JAGUAR

is the largest cat in the
Americas. Its coat is
normally yellow and
tan. The jaguar has a
compact body, a broad
head and powerful
jaws.

ATLANTIC GHOST CRAB

is a common species along the Atlantic coast of the United States. This crab can produce a variety of sound by striking the ground with the claw, by stridulation with the legs, and an incompletely explained bubbling sound .

BANANA SLUG

are often yellow in color and are sometimes spotted with brown, like a ripe or overripe banana. Banana slugs are detritivores, or decomposers. They process leaves, animal droppings, moss, and dead plant material, and then recycle them into soil humus.

ALBINO BURMESE PYTHON

are white with patterns in butterscotch yellow and burnt orange. The Burmese python is one of the five largest snakes in the world.

GOLDENROD CRAB SPIDER

is the largest and best-known flower spider in North America. These spiders may be yellow or white, depending on the flower in which they are hunting. These spiders are sometimes called banana spiders because of their striking yellow color.

LABIDOCHROMIS CAERULEUS

is also known as lemon yellow lab, the blue streak hap, the electric yellow or yellow prince, depending on the colour morph. This species is a maternal mouthbrooder, meaning the eggs are carried, hatch, and develop in the mother s mouth for about three weeks.

BRAIN CORAL

are found in shallow warm-water coral reefs in all the world s oceans. The lifespan of the largest brain corals is 900 years. Brain corals extend their tentacles to catch food at night. During the day, they use their tentacles for protection by wrapping them over the grooves on their surface.

YELLOW SEAHORSE

is a small, equine-like fish, with extraordinary breeding methods. The male carries the eggs in a brood pouch on his lower abdomen. To give birth , the male bends forwards and then backwards, thrusting his pouch forward expelling one or two youngsters with explosive force.

www.ingramcontent.com/pod-product-compliance
Lightning Source LLC
Chambersburg PA
CBHW080947130726
48003CB00010BA/3129